Single
GOD
Life

Image inspiration
for the
Saved & Single

MARCUS GILL

Single God Life. Image Inspiration for the Saved and Single.

Scriptures marked NIV are taken from the NEW INTERNATIONAL VERSION (NIV): Scripture taken from THE HOLY BIBLE, NEW INTERNATIONAL VERSION ®. Copyright© 1973, 1978, 1984, 2011 by Biblica, Inc.TM. Used by permission of Zondervan

Marcus Gill International

PO BOX 16124

West Haven, Connecticut 06516

MARCUS GILL
INTERNATIONAL

To Zealiah Crystal Gill,

My beautiful beloved daughter.

Continue to rest in paradise.

THE SINGLE GOD LIFE IS ABOUT KNOWING THAT YOU ARE STRONG, NOT PHYSICALLY BUT EMOTIONALLY STRONG. YOU KNOW WHO YOU ARE BECAUSE YOU BELIEVE THAT THE GLORY OF GOD DWELLS INSIDE OF YOU. YOU KNOW HOW TO WAIT. YOU KNOW HOW TO WORSHIP. THEREFORE, YOU KNOW HOW TO WIN!

Having been gifted with the ability to create inspirational word graphics, I decided to start creating posts for Facebook that would encourage singles. My focus is not only on Christian singles; actually, I concentrate on all people who have been in bad relationships, and also those who are preparing for new relationships. Most of my graphic inspirational quotes are inspired by my very own personal experiences in relationships. These are not just good ideas. These are real life thoughts that I wish would have been spoken to me before I made some of the worst decisions of my life! *Important to listen.*

The truth of the matter is, we all get warnings before we make major choices. Sometimes the warnings come from family and friends. Other times, the warnings come from people that you really do not trust. As I look back over my life, I can never say that I was not given a heads up that I was about to make a major FAIL! I thank God that He opened doors of escape for me so that I could continue to live and do His work. Moreover, I am able to help warn others. By reading my graphic quotes and the statements that accompany some, you will get a simple warning of certain things to watch for so that you do not end up miserable in the wrong relationship. *If we desire a fulfilling, God-led, and blissful relationship, we MUST want what God wants, not what our flesh desires.* *It's not all about the human desire*

Repeat these victorious affirmations every day as you rededicate your focus to God in this, your season of waiting on the mate He has chosen for you: "I wait,

Declare this over my life daily.

meaning I am willing to live and enjoy my time of singleness until God sends my mate. I worship, meaning I will remain focused, while loving and serving God. I will continually be praying, fasting and worshipping the Lord, while hearing His voice guiding my footsteps." Waiting on God and worshipping God with our whole hearts will guarantee our victory! You are certainly going to WIN!

Don't let negativity to be the only catalist for Change

Do not allow your rough experiences to be the only reasons why you decide to work on your patience. Sadly, this has been the story of my life: Going through the worst of the worst and then realizing the value of being single. At the same time, I am grateful for the bad experiences because they made me stronger. They gave me a testimony, and now I can pass along some simple yet powerful advice. My encouragement has gone from social media to this book. Let this simple but powerful read inspire you!

FOR A SEASON YOU MAY HAVE TO DANCE ALONE TO THE RHYTHM OF YOUR HEARTBEAT.

MARCUSGILL.ORG

1

DANCE ALONE

The feeling of being alone is not always pleasurable. Naturally, we want to be around someone we enjoy. We like to mingle with people who have like interests. To meet someone who enjoys exactly what you enjoy would be a miracle. You would get to have a blast together! Sounds exciting, right? It is. The only bad news is right now, you don't have the benefit of enjoying that special someone. Do not allow yourself to fall into a place of sadness because your party has no attendee. It is ok to stay home on a weekend evening and enjoy your alone time.

If you only understood, the value of your "You Time," you would not be in a rush to create a load of your own personal party invitations. You know you best. You know you better than anyone else knows you. There is no body on this planet that could describe you like you. You know what makes you happy. You know what makes you angry. Have you ever wondered why it seems like nobody can make you happy? Perhaps it is because you are depending too much on others to please you and satisfy you. You must adjust to your own rhythm. You can search all over the world and you will never find anyone to satisfy your lonely dance if you do not learn how to enjoy the dance alone!

Even as good and self-worthy as it sounds, sometimes the dance alone season is for God to do some cleaning up as well. There are some things that are in you that God needs to clean out before He sends you that special someone. We do not want to ever carry past pains into a new relationship. We do not need to bring old trash into a new treasure box. So, God will allow us to be in a season of dancing alone until our dance floor is ready for His dance partner. You never want to rush out of one bad experience and hop into a new one so quickly. Let God do His work in you for a season. You can still

Don't depend on others to make you happy

enjoy this season. God's waiting time is not always punishment time. He wants you to wait, worship, and win. That is more than enough reason to dance! Rejoice now over what God is doing and going to do just for you. As you rejoice, know that you are giving God a pre-meditated praise for a post-dated miracle. Your heart will be your soundtrack. It is the proof that you are waiting and you are still alive!

I challenge you to take a moment and reflect on the great things that you have accomplished. Think about the many trials that you've stood through and won. Think about the abuse (emotionally, physically, or spiritually) that you have survived. When you reflect on the greatness that is in you, you will begin to glee over your own self-worth, and you will begin to celebrate all by yourself. Your heart should have been broken and destroyed by now, knowing what you have faced in your past; yet, it is still beating. Dance to that sound. It is the sound of life. Everyone cannot team up with your celebration just yet. You have to know that others may come along and not appreciate your history. To avoid that disappointment, learn how to encourage yourself, by yourself. Laugh alone. Cry alone. Party alone. Your God sent mate will join in with no hesitation. When you build your self-esteem high, you will understand that a good time in life does not require help. Your future mate will just enhance your joyful experience. Do not wait for your mate to show up before you start your life celebration. Start celebrating now; and then, if they are worthy enough, just invite them to the party!

Bible Reference:

Deuteronomy 31:6 Be strong and courageous. Do not fear or tremble before them, for the Lord your God is the one who is going with you. He will not fail you or abandon you!

↳ Joshua had to go it alone for a season so that he would make a way for what was to come in the future. He was faithful to what God had on his life and made a way for others.

YOUR GOD SENT MATE WILL NEVER EMBARRASS YOU ON PURPOSE.

MARCUSGILL.ORG

2

NO HUMILIATION

Your reputation is important. As you stand alone for the time being, you are solely responsible for your own image. The truth is, it's up to you, and only you, to maintain a good reputation. As a single person, you have total control over what you do behind closed doors or in public before the eyes of many. The choices that you make alone can make your name great or make your name negative. Maintaining a good reputation is easy to do when you are a God fearing, single individual.

When you walk alone, those who wish to judge you (good or bad) will only see and judge you. When you decide to commit to a potential mate, you better be quick to identify, embarrassing personality traits. If you connect with someone without carefully examining their behavior, you put yourself at risk of losing you positive reputation. Everyone who behaves polite in private will not be polite in public. Be careful not to commit to a person who is good at "acting" civilized. The real monster will eventually come out. When you have a real relationship with God, you will activate your gift to discern those things that are simply not right. Don't ignore it!

If it doesn't feel right — it isn't

Your God-sent mate will not overlook your progress in life. The special individual for you will not ignore the steps that you have been taking to maintain a great reputation for yourself. They will recognize your effort to walk in excellence. You may be the type of person who lives a life for the sake of others. You may be a representative of your church, community group, or school; in your world, your reputation counts. Your God sent mate will be one who honors that. They know that the two of you walking together is no longer about individual judgment; it is about how you will be judged together.

Furthermore, be extremely aware of the traits of a jealous person. You have worked hard. You are almost at the point of being satisfied with your accomplishments. You can lose it all if you find yourself in this guileless position. You are unaware of this person's jealousy towards you. This evil spirit will rise in public places. They will fall in love with your life, but secretly they will try to imperceptibly embarrass you in the presence of others just to see you fail. Trust me, you will pick up on these hidden traits during private conversations about your success. When you ask for their participation or support for a public event or gathering, notice how they respond. Notice how they fight against the expectations of excellence. Rebel-spirited people most commonly embarrass the dignified people around them.

Based upon personal experience, I can tell you it does not feel good at all. You can be connected to someone who could care less what people think about you. I can remember being ordained as an Elder in the Lord's church. The person who I expected to participate and walk with me in excellence absolutely rebelled against what was expected as a sign of obedience to the presentation of this sacred ceremony. I stood out as the odd ball amongst my peers because of that purposeful embarrassment. I can even remember a time when I was scheduled to preach and I had to try to minister through the evil looks and even the loud and obnoxious behavior of my partner at the time. In moments like these, you can only cover your face and make constant apologies to maintain peace; but it does not always work. Committing to people like this will burn bridges in your life. Avoid being humiliated. Your God-sent mate will make sure your reputation is one to always be admired.

Bible Reference:

Ecclesiastes 7:1 A good reputation is better than precious perfume; likewise, the day of one's death is better than the day of one's birth.

Always try to live a life that is above repute, ensure that if anyone tried to make allegations against me they would not be believed.

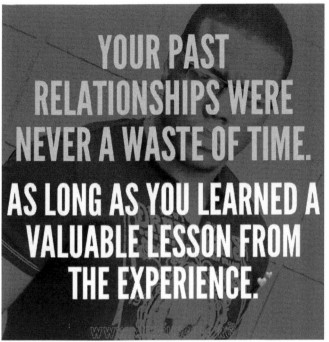

YOUR PAST
RELATIONSHIPS WERE
NEVER A WASTE OF TIME.
AS LONG AS YOU LEARNED A
VALUABLE LESSON FROM
THE EXPERIENCE.

♥ Remember this

3

NO TIME WASTED

For the most part, no sensible human being wants to re-live an ugly past. In fact, if it was not for the sake of sharing the testimony of our past to benefit someone else, we would avoid talking about it. We do not like to allow our minds to reflect on the disappointments of our yesterday. Most of us try our best to forget about the horrible experiences that we have had in previous relationships. We must realize forgiving does not mean forgetting; forgiveness means freedom.

The best position to be in mentally, when it pertains to reflecting on our past, is knowing that our pain was for a purpose. No pain means no gain. There are so many people who have lost their minds going through some of the things that you went through. Some people have committed suicide because the experience was too hard for them to handle. You made it through. Why? There was a lesson in your storm that God needed to teach you. Sometimes we place ourselves in these types of situations. We know better, yet we allow our flesh to place us in these positions. Once we get settled in our fleshly place, the truth behind why you should have avoided this begins to manifest itself. Now you need a way of escape. This is when we begin to utter the words "I wish I would have never done this!" If you have ever heard yourself say these words, chances are, you are learning a lesson.

As you prepare for your God-sent mate, you will reflect on your past experiences. When you have had a rough relationship before, you are enabled to see, recognize, and identify faultiness quicker. Thanks to the relationships that failed before, you now know how to say no early and not waste so much time again. When you rushed into it before, you will now not rush into a new relationship. When you laid down and gave your body away to an uncommitted

The lesson that I am not God, I cannot do things in my own strength

Take time, there is no rush, it will happen in its own time.

friend before, you will refuse to surrender so quickly again (especially without a marital covenant).

In this new season of your life, you will not repeat the same mistakes. You will not go back. You will not go in circles, expecting to have a great life. It is time to move forward. Do not disregard what you have been through. Reflect back on the mistakes you have made and remember the pain of that experience; do not repeat it. Know that your past relationship(s) were not a waste. If you learned a valuable lesson from the experience, it worked for the good of your future. You may have been lied to, lied on, used and abused; but, it was not a waste. Now you know what to avoid in the future. You will never waste time learning a lesson while you could be learning how to love. Never forget the lessons of your past pain.

When I think about my own testimony, I realize that all of the pain that I have endured from past relationships made me stronger. It caused me to learn how to be patient. I have learned how to be obedient to the voice of God. The pain of my past has turned me in the direction to always seek God before making a commitment to anything in life (not just relationships). I often testify that I would not be the strong man that I am now if it had not been for a few bumps and bruises along the way. I encourage you never regret any experience in life. Just know that this next time around you will be totally surrendered

I will NOT go back.

to God and you will be able to help someone else avoid the painful experience(s) that you have faced. Not only do you get to learn from your past, but you get to become a teacher too!

Bible Reference:

Romans 8:28 And we know that all things work together for good for those who love God, who are called according to his purpose.

All things help us get to where we are meant to be, even if we take a detour along the way.

YOU ARE ALONE
FOR A REASON
GOD IS PREPARING
YOU FOR A
DRAMA FREE FUTURE!

www.marcusall.org

4

DRAMA FREE LIFE

As I think about the things that I love and enjoy, one of the things that stand out is peace. I love peace of mind. I love peaceful atmospheres. I love peaceful conversations. I love peaceful people. On the contrary, I absolutely hate drama! When I speak of drama, I am not speaking of the artistic and creative performance of an actor or actress. I define drama as a way of relating to the world by consistently overreacting to or greatly exaggerating the importance of benign events. In other words, I cannot stand wasting time on things that do not deserve so much emotion and attention. I am sure you totally agree with this statement, "Drama is not welcome in my life. Drama, keep out!"

This season of your life has been one of waiting. You are waiting alone. You have the desire to connect with someone that you can enjoy life with but it seems like it is taking forever. Understand this: God could allow just anybody to come in to your life at any moment but He will not. He is preparing the best for you. God already knows that you cannot stand fussing, arguing, and reasoning about things that should not matter to adults. Perhaps all of the people that are close to you carry some load of drama: those people who are super sensitive; those people who overreact to everything! You may even be considering someone at this point, but God will not allow you to commit to them because He already knows that this person is carrying a lot of baggage. God wants you to have a drama free relationship.

Furthermore, you must understand that some people carry drama that does not even pertain to them. So, imagine you rushing into a relationship without getting to know your potential mates' family members and friends. That is one of the saddest experiences for an individual to have to go though. I have been through it myself. I have learned that you cannot be a peace making super hero either. You will fail every time (especially if you are not a drama-filled person). I was there. Trying to be everyone else's savior will cause you to lose your mind with them. You will miss the valuable moments. Here you are trying to love this person, yet you have to deal with all of the drama that comes with their family and friends. When you could be out for a nice dinner and a movie, you are riding over to their family's house everyday trying to smile through family disputes. You do not have time for the drama. You may even have a situation whereas your potential mate still has connections to their ex. That is the absolute worst for anybody. You are trying to fall in love with a new person that you think God sent into your life and their crazy and deranged ex is stalking you both. What a headache right? You do not have time for that.

Be patient. Wait for God to do what He does best. He will send the right person to cross your path. They will not be carrying old drama-filled dead weight. They will be strong and independent. They will not allow the mess of those around them, from neither present nor past relationships, to distract what it is that God is doing for you both. In fact, your God-sent mate will protect you from any and everything that could be a disturbance to the healthy relationship that you both are trying to build. So wait. Wait for God to send that special person into your life. You will not have to endure the agony of wasting your valuable life time on messy things that have nothing to do with you. Prepare for your drama free future!

Bible Reference:

1 Thessalonians 4:11-12 Aspire to lead a quiet life, to attend to your own business, and to work with your own hands, as we commanded you. In this way you will live a decent life before outsiders and not be in need.

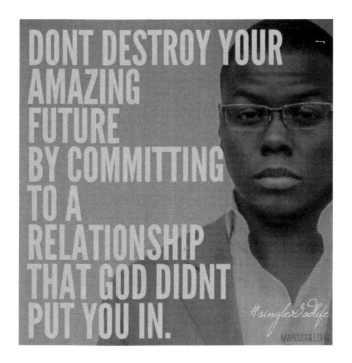

DONT DESTROY YOUR AMAZING FUTURE BY COMMITTING TO A RELATIONSHIP THAT GOD DIDNT PUT YOU IN.

#singleGodlife

MARCUSGILL.ORG

5

NO HUMILIATION

There is an old song that I remember the saints singing in church when I was younger. They sang, "I got just what I wanted from the Lord!" It is such a great blessing when we receive the blessings of God. Knowing that what we have received in life came from heaven above will cause great celebration. There is a question that comes to mind during these types of celebrations. Did God really do this? Or, did I do this myself? There are so many people who are in committed relationships that God did not arrange.

Most relationships that experience more trouble than peace, if not all of them, are most likely functioning without the hand of God. When God does not ordain a relationship, you cannot expect God to bless it. We walk by faith and not by sight. Therefore, we believe by faith that God will orchestrate and connect us with the right person. When we are letting God lead, we do not trust in orchestrating and connecting ourselves. We must let God do the work. When He works, we must know it is Him.

Your future is blessed. Your future is full of prosperity and joy. Your future is filled with peace and good health. God also has a relationship in store for you that will guarantee everlasting joy for you. Do not miss this great blessing of your future because you decide to make a commitment without knowing that God ordained it. So many people end up committing themselves to someone because of their own fleshly desires. Everything that looks good is not of God. You have dreams. You have goals. You have a vision. Do not allow yourself to fall into a man-made relationship that will distract you from achieving the amazing goals that you have longed to complete. When you connect to the wrong person, God will hold back the blessings that He has for you. There are people in this world that do not deserve the blessings that God has for you. Your blessed future can and will be foiled when you ignore the voice of God and go after what you want. Temporary satisfaction can destroy your eternal joy. What do you care about more? Your right now? Or your eternity? Anybody can make you happy for a moment, but will that happiness last? You must make up in your mind that God has too many great things in store for you. You must not allow man to impress you with momentary pleasure which can turn into long term pain. Everyone cannot enter into the favor of the Lord with you. You have been focused on God: Praying, fasting, worshipping, giving, and living holy has been your lifestyle. Do not get distracted. Do not abort the delivery of your package of Glory. You have an inheritance and you must be in God's will to receive it. If God is not in it, you will miss it.

Can you imagine all of the connections that God wants to make for you? Can you envision all the people that God has already arranged to cross your path to benefit you? What if you connect with the wrong person and they ruin your opportunity by being rude or not knowing how to behave properly in great places. As I stated in a previous section of this book, being with the wrong person can burn bridges or block you from reaching the bridge you need to cross. I can tell you, if God had not created a way of escape for me from a previous relationship, I would not be able to function and bless so many lives as I do now. We must stay connected to heaven in order to avoid connecting to a hindrance.

There is good news to be known! God will speak to you and show you who is for you. God will open your ears to hear and your eyes to see. He will open your heart to know and understand that He approves. Your God-sent mate will be qualified to enjoy the blessings of your future. Let God work it out. He never fails.

Bible Reference:

Jeremiah 29:11 For I know what I have planned for you,' says the Lord. 'I have plans to prosper you, not to harm you. I have plans to give you a future filled with hope.

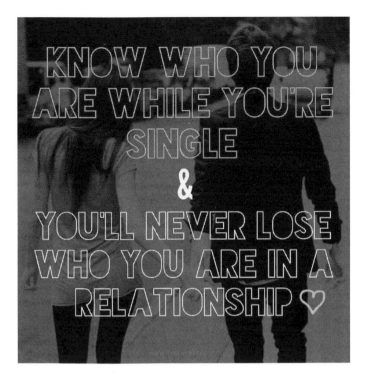

KNOW WHO YOU ARE WHILE YOU'RE SINGLE & YOU'LL NEVER LOSE WHO YOU ARE IN A RELATIONSHIP ♡

6

I KNOW WHO I AM

You must know who you are. Do you know yourself? It is very important that you know your own self-worth before you commit to a relationship. You have to be confident in yourself now. You do not want to commit to a relationship and end up losing your own identity. When you know who you are first, no one else can ruin your view of how awesome you are. Identify your greatness, and then your God-sent mate will do the same.

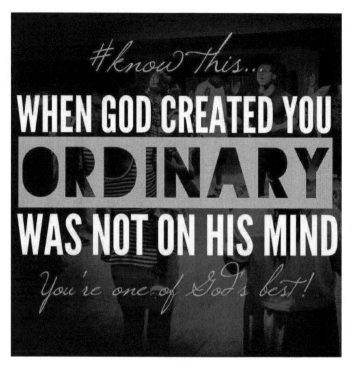

#knowThis...
WHEN GOD CREATED YOU
ORDINARY
WAS NOT ON HIS MIND
You're one of God's best!

7

EXTRAORDINARY

When God created you, He had the greatest idea in mind. God did not create you to be regular. God made you to be extraordinary. The Bible says that greater is He that is in us! You are not average, ordinary, or normal; but, you are beyond normal! Your God-sent mate will not be ordinary either. You both will be an extraordinary team!

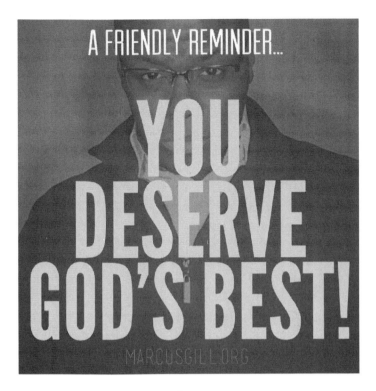

A FRIENDLY REMINDER...

YOU DESERVE GOD'S BEST!

MARCUSGILL.ORG

8

YOU ARE ONE OF HIS FAVORITES.

You do not need to forfeit the mighty gifts and blessings that come with you being a child of God. Do not rush god and settle for less. You are not a child of God to go through life settling for just enough. You deserve God's best because you are fathered by the best. You are a King's kid. Just be reminded, you better not settle for anything other than God's best.

MARCUSGILL.ORG

9

REAL LOVE IS SEARCHING FOR YOU.

Are you searching for love? Are you seeking beyond desperation? I have good news for you. As you are reading this text, there is an amazing amount of God-influenced love looking for you. The very love that you want to give is searching for your heart. Your God-sent mate is on the way, preparing to be your greatest friend first.

10

BENEFITS ARE FOR THOSE WHO QUALIFY.

You are royalty! Please do not ever forget that. When someone comes into your life and does a few nice things for you, you must not get overly excited and release all of your treasures to them. Everybody is not worth your life and the glorious things that come with you. They must pay for that. Take your time and wait to see if your potential mate is worth sharing your kingdom with. Their long-term sacrifice for you matters.

WHEN YOU WATER DOWN YOUR TRUE SELF FOR A RELATIONSHIP YOU WASTE YOUR GOD GIVEN VALUE AND YOULL ALWAYS BE MISERABLE

Don't settle. Wait!

11

WALK IN YOUR GREATNESS.

There is greatness in you. You must realize and understand this about yourself or no one else will. When you were born, something special was birthed into the world with you. For the most part, as you grow up you are also discovering what your purpose in life will be. Throughout life, you discover your gifts and talents. You learn people skills and you connect with other people who have the same interests. We may not like to admit it, but every so often we find ourselves competing with others and this causes problems. But, it is not always a bad thing. It just makes you work harder and it helps you to realize your worth and level of ability. The best thing about it is you get to learn you. When you know who you are, you live with confidence knowing that you can and will be the greatest you that has ever lived. The bad news is everybody cannot handle the value of you.

As you prepare for your God-sent mate, you must remember who you are. Do not ever get to a place where you care more about the feelings of another person and forget about yourself. Unfortunately, there will be some who will be interested in you because of how they feel being with you will benefit them. Deep down on the inside of their soul, they really cannot handle it. Your personality may be too big for them. You may be too beautiful or too handsome. Your education, experience, and creativity may exceed their level of thinking. When it comes to spiritual things, the anointing on your life may intimidate them. If you get connected to this kind of person, you are in trouble.

My experience in a bad relationship can help me teach you a great lesson. When you connect with someone who cannot handle the magnitude of who you are, they will imperceptibly try to belittle who you really are. They will complain about your greatness. This type of person will make attempts to encourage you to "slow down" or "take a break"; and if you get a really bold one, they will try and find ways to get you to quit. This is what I mean when I say "water down"; when you try to minimize yourself for someone else, you take the real spice out of who you are.

Can you imagine being in a relationship where you cannot be yourself? Your mate will complain everyday about your success. This comes of course from the spirit of jealousy and competition. Here is the trap: you try so hard to make your mate happy and you end up hiding your true self and instead becoming who they want you to be. This will make your life miserable. No one wants to be in a box. Do not allow yourself to commit to someone who shows signs of control and selfishness. They will try and box you in and you will never reach your full potential. The Lord has blessed you with remarkable gifts and abilities. You carry yourself with excellence and everyone recognizes it. You are anointed and called by God to do great exploits for His kingdom. Do not waste your God given potential by taking a seat to satisfy the insecurities of another. While you are courting, take notice of these signs. Words like, "Can you tone it down?" or "That's too much" or "Why do you have to be so good?" should be deal breakers! (Especially when you know you are doing what God has called you to do).

There are no limits with God. Your God-sent mate will embrace who you are. They will enhance the real you. He or She will not try and devalue your dreams. Your personality will be enjoyed and accepted. The gifts of the spirit that operate in your life will be embraced and cultivated. Your efforts to be successful will not be criticized. You will not be miserable because you will always be encouraged.

Bible Reference:

Psalms 27:1-2 The Lord delivers and vindicates me! I fear no one! The Lord protects my life! I am afraid of no one! When evil men attack me to devour my flesh, when my adversaries and enemies attack me, they stumble and fall.

YOUR GOD FEARING
STRONG
UNSELFISH
SECURE
CONFIDENT
HONEST - LOVING
AND FAITHFUL MATE WILL BE
REVEALED WHEN
GOD SAYS ITS TIME!

<u>12</u>

WAITING FOR THE REVELATION

Waiting on God is not always easy. We have so many desires, dreams, and images in our mind. We want to see these dreams come to pass. When it comes to our plans of being married and committed to that special someone, we hope for the absolute best. Most of us get extra anxious when we think of our future relationship, but we have to pump the brakes. It is ok to be excited about your heart's desires being fulfilled, but you must be willing and ready to wait on God. Your waiting prepares you to win God's best.

You want a strong mate. You want someone who is able to not just exhibit great physical power, but more importantly one who has moral and intellectual power. That special someone must think on your level and even greater. They must be unselfish. What a great miracle it would be for you to have a strong minded mate who is willing to put your needs before their own. That person must be one who is willing and ready to love you with all that they have. You must be ready to do the same. You cannot pray for an unselfish mate and you have selfish issues yourself. That just would not be fair. Along with them being strong and unselfish, you want them to be secure with themselves. Can you imagine two unselfish and confident people together in a relationship? Now that is what you call a power couple! You have got to believe that is in your future. One of the greatest prayer requests of them all, when it comes to prayers for your future mate, is that they must be honest. No man or woman in their right mind wants to be committed to a liar. Honesty is important.

To meet someone who is strong, unselfish, secure, confident and honest would be the answer to millions of single individuals' prayers. These character traits and many more are most certainly possible. You must decree and declare that you refuse to settle for anything less than Godly excellence. To use your imagination and rejoice over the good idea of this mate showing up into your life is easy. Waiting for God to reveal him or her can be extremely painful. The truth of the matter is, God has to reveal them to you first before you can even accept them. God will show you who they are and then give you the time to evaluate them for yourself. But you cannot force yourself into believing that someone is carrying the traits that you have been praying for. You cannot see the faults and ignore them because you are in such a big rush to be in a relationship. Do not try to make your own revelation happen. You will fail. You will be miserable for the rest of your life if you make a commitment based on the potential you see in someone and not who they actually are now. People can perfectly fake character traits. Do not allow yourself to make a decision based upon a flesh revelation. You must allow God to reveal the truth.

There were times in my own life when I made attempts to fake the revelation. You can be dating someone and see that the character qualities of that individual are not at the level that you desire. Instead of making the decision to part ways, you will find yourself overlooking the reality of that person and making excuses for them. When you do this, you lose valuable time in life. You will not fully enjoy what you make happen in your own time. You must let God's timing be your timing.

When God is ready for you to see your prayers answered, He will show Himself strong and mighty in your life. When you meet the special person that God has for you, you will never doubt or question if it is God or not. You will know. You will not have to ignore or fake satisfaction. Wait for God's time.

Bible Reference:

Habakkuk 2:3 For the message is a witness to what is decreed; it gives reliable testimony about how matters will turn out. Even if the message is not fulfilled right away, wait patiently; for it will certainly come to pass—it will not arrive late.

YOUR FUTURE MATE MUST RECOGNIZE AND OBEY THE VOICE OF GOD JUST LIKE YOU.

MARCUSGILL.ORG

13

KNOW GOD THE SAME

As Christians, we are taught that we need to marry someone who has the same relationship with God that we have. We are taught that two coming together who are unequally yoked simply means that someone in the relationship is not saved and the other is a devout dedicated Christian. We are warned that making a decision to commit to this type of relationship will land us in a place of misery.

As a result of such warnings, we purposefully pursue someone who is fully involved in ministry. We seek for someone who is spiritually-oriented. When we meet someone and they are easy to look at, have a great personality, and we find out that they are claiming salvation, we get excited. We feel as if our prayers have been answered. The cherry on top in these cases is the claim of salvation. One would say, "Yes, they are saved, therefore we are equally yoked." However, we must understand that just because someone says they are saved does not mean that their personal relationship with God is equally yoked with yours. People see God differently. The way you interpret scriptures may be different than your potential mate's way of understanding the word. You may meet someone who is radical for God like you are, but you must take your time to get to know the other person's relationship with God. If you do not take your time, you will find yourself having arguments about your Godly passion.

To meet someone in church is great. Seeing someone worshipping God and operating in their spiritual gifts does spike interest. That is only what you see on the outside of an individual. That always looks good to our eyes. It is much deeper than that. You will begin to discover the true thoughts of a person once you begin to have conversations with them outside of the public worship setting.

The best way to learn how your potential mate hears from God is to have discussions about scripture. If you feel as if certain behavior is not right in the sight of God and your potential mate disagrees, that is a sure sign that they do not hear from God like you do. This does not always mean you are always correct, but it does mean that the two of you do not see eye to eye. When you find yourself arguing over the interpretation of God's word, you are in a bad position. I have had this experience before of thinking that I could convince the opposite party to see the word like I see it. It does not work. You will know right away that there is a disconnection or misunderstanding of viewpoints. For two Christians who think they have the potential of being together, it is not a good idea to continue dating when it is already obvious that you do not hear from God the same way. That will do nothing but create more confusion and headache, especially for you if you have a great vision or assignment for the Kingdom of God.

With God, all things are possible, so this means that there is someone out there who does know God like you. As you continue to wait on God, in due season you are going to meet someone who loves the Lord like you. They are obedient to the whole truth of God's word like you. You will see eye to eye when it comes to your assignment. There will be no arguments over God's word or even the application of the word to your lives. I have experienced a relationship where my partner fought against everything good that God revealed was. It's a miserable experience. God will bless you with that special someone who will support your God-given goals. They will recognize the voice of God like you. Instead of questioning the glory on your life they will be anxious to be your teammate and help you achieve everything that God has called you to do. In the name of Jesus!

Bible Reference:

2 Corinthians 6:14 Do not become partners with those who do not believe, for what partnership is there between righteousness and lawlessness, or what fellowship does light have with darkness?

14

I REFUSE TO BE ABUSED.

You can never make the mistake of interpreting love the wrong way. This subject makes me angry more than anything else. There are so many kind, friendly, and loving people in relationships that are the opposite of what they deserve. I can remember a situation that I in which I placed myself. I had committed myself to a relationship knowing that the opposite party had some serious issues. I covered them. I ignored what I knew was wrong because I thought that my love for this particular person would help them to heal. I ended up spending two years of my life tolerating abuse, thinking that is was the right thing to do because I loved her. I found out that it was just getting worse and it would never get better. Do not allow yourself to become connected with someone so intensely that you end up being passive of the pain that they are putting you through. It will destroy you. When someone purposefully allows themselves to put you through unnecessary pain that they know you do not deserve, they are abusing you. Most of us who have kind hearts go through this in many ways. It is not love, it is attention-seeking behavior. You do not deserve this.

When we hear the word abuse, especially when it pertains to relationships, our first thought is physical abuse. As serious as physical abuse is, it is not the only form of abuse. Furthermore, physical abuse is not the worst form of abuse either. One can be abused mentally, emotionally, and spiritually. Have you ever been spoken to the wrong way and it really hurt? That is mental abuse. I want you to know and understand that as you are allowing God to direct your path, you do not deserve to be spoken to disrespectfully. During your dating season, you better recognize right away if your momentary potential mate has an abusive tongue. The first time you have to surprisingly reply with an urban, "Excuse me?" yea, it is time to move on. Anyone who wants to journey through courtship with you better speak with respect.

Regarding emotional abuse, I have had a bad experience with being emotionally abused. This is when the opposite party purposely says things to you to destroy your heart. When you notice that they play with their words concerning things that have emotional value in your heart, you know that this person is trying to emotionally abuse you. Conversations will spring up from their mouth concerning things that they know will make you jealous or even make you cry because they know it will hurt you. You do not deserve it.

Spiritual abuse does not pertain too much to relationships. Although it does creep its way in at times, it is normally not at the forefront of abuse between a romantically involved couple. Spiritual abuse comes against those who are dedicated to God. People who want to take advantage of you because of it will try to get you to please them by shadowing your fear of God. This is when the opposite party will make attempts to use the Word of God against you to make their cause correct to control you. Do not allow yourself to be manipulated into someone else's world of action because they rearrange your view of God and who He has called you to be.

God has a mate for you who will not abuse you. They will not take advantage of you. They will not abuse you. God will not allow you to commit to an abusive relationship without warning you. He will show you signs. He will speak to you. You must not ignore his voice. If you are being abused now, don't you dare for one second confuse it with love. It is not love. It is control. It is manipulation and it is not of God.

Bible Reference:

Proverbs 22:10 Drive out the scorner and contention will leave; strife and insults will cease.

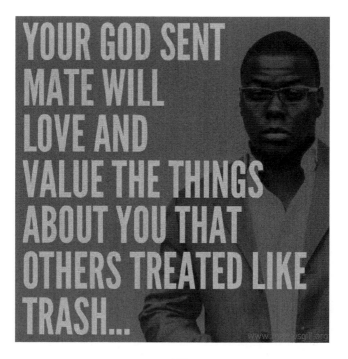

YOUR GOD SENT MATE WILL LOVE AND VALUE THE THINGS ABOUT YOU THAT OTHERS TREATED LIKE TRASH...

15

ALWAYS VALUABLE

Your God-sent mate will love you. That is the most important action on their part. If you find yourself making a commitment to someone whom you can obviously see does not really love you, you are knowingly setting yourself up for romantic failure. When you have a true relationship with God, you should automatically be able to recognize real love. The truth is, there are so many great characteristics that you possess. I would even be bold enough to say that there are amazing things about you that you have not even discovered about yourself yet. That is just how amazing God is. When He created you, He had no limits. He made you awesome. Your God-sent mate will not ignore the amazing attributes of your make-up. Unfortunately, there are people who will cross our paths and be unappreciative of the value that God has given us. You do not need to waste your time committing to someone who does not love and appreciate all of you.

When I reflect on my own relationship experience, I can assuredly tell you how painful it is to be unappreciated. The feeling of being treated like trash just for doing the right thing will make you want to lose your mind. Thank God I did not. I did everything in the world (that I knew was possible) to put a smile on her face. Nothing was ever good enough. Even in the moments when I thought that I had won, there was still some fault found in the good. The frustration will literally began to make you feel as if you yourself are crazy. I thank God for the Holy Spirit. God continued to remind me that the value in me was so great, that small minds will not be able to receive or comprehend my worth. As you read this, I want you to know the same. Your self-worth and value is so awesome and it is going to take more than a small minded, ungrateful, and unappreciative person to be your mate. Your God-sent mate will be equipped to handle and appreciate the true value of you. You may have been in a previous relationship where you have given your all and it seemed as if giving your all was worthless. If these are the thoughts that you have had concerning yourself, please erase those thoughts. This is how Satan convinces us to change who we are. When you give our all just to get slapped in the face for being real, nice, loving and Godly kind, it will make you want to change. You will be tempted to say, "I'm not being nice anymore" or "I am tired of always being truthful and getting hurt". Do not take on this mindset. If you let go of the valuable characteristics you have, you will not be able to enjoy your God-sent mate. You must be compatible with that special person that God is going to send into your life. They will appreciate who you are. They will not discourage you from being yourself. The very things that your last mate treated like trash, your God-sent mate will treat like treasure. Your days of being mistreated, used, and abused, are over. Your God-sent mate will not take advantage of you. They will be anxious to enhance you.

You must not get discouraged. You must not change because of bitterness. Those bad experiences that you have had in the past were only to make you stronger. The pain was to help you see the value of having God in you. When you change who you are, you will miss out on the benefits that come as a result of your God given personality. What a beautiful feeling it is to know that God has someone in existence with your same attitude and your same spirit. They value the same things that you value. They will not belittle the things that you see. Your future plans, dreams, and visions will be supported and not mocked. Prepare for that special someone who will love and value the things that you almost gave up on. You will know that you are treasured.

Bible Reference:

Colossians 3:12-14 Therefore, as the elect of God, holy and dearly loved, clothe yourselves with a heart of mercy, kindness, humility, gentleness, and patience, bearing with one another and forgiving one another, if someone happens to have a complaint against anyone else. Just as the Lord has forgiven you, so you also forgive others. And to all these virtues add love, which is the perfect bond.

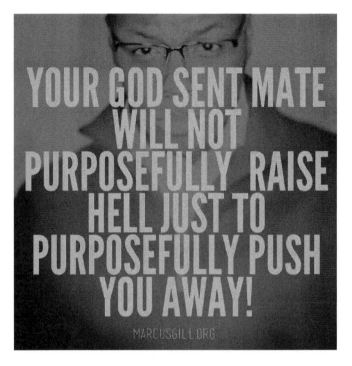

YOUR GOD SENT MATE WILL NOT PURPOSEFULLY RAISE HELL JUST TO PURPOSEFULLY PUSH YOU AWAY!

MARCUSGILL.ORG

16

THEY REALLY WANT YOU.

God will never send you someone who does not really appreciate you. I have had a horrible experience in this area. Being in a relationship where your partner does evil things to purposely frustrate you is a miserable thing. Your God sent mate will do everything in the world to make sure you never leave. They will not give you Hell to get you to depart. They will love you above and beyond because that want you.

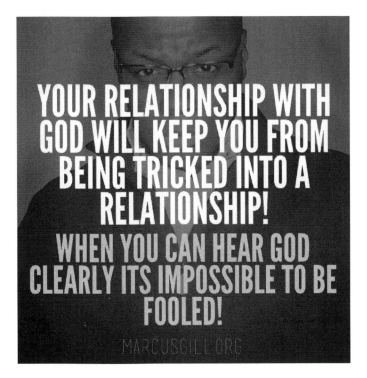

YOUR RELATIONSHIP WITH GOD WILL KEEP YOU FROM BEING TRICKED INTO A RELATIONSHIP! WHEN YOU CAN HEAR GOD CLEARLY ITS IMPOSSIBLE TO BE FOOLED!

MARCUSGILL.ORG

17

TRUTH OVER TRICKS

One of the greatest gifts from God is having the ability to hear and recognize His voice. This is why it is important to have and maintain a real relationship with God. When you are dating, you must be in tuned to God's voice. It is ok to be in love or highly interested in a person but you must not lose your connection with God. He will speak to you and reveal to you warnings of destruction. He will never let you fail. You will not be fooled.

YOUR GOD SENT MATE WILL KNOW WHEN YOURE HURTING WITHOUT YOU SAYING IT.

MARCUSGILL.ORG

18

THE ABILITY TO HEAR YOUR HEART

Sometimes talking does not work. Communication is a very important part of being in a relationship, especially when you are just dating. A true sign of someone being connected to your heart, is when they know when you are hurting without you verbally expressing it. God will send you someone who is more interested in your inside that your outward appearance.

WHEN YOU BRING PAST RELATIONSHIP DRAMA INTO YOUR NEW RELATIONSHIP YOU POISON YOUR POTENTIAL OF EXPERIENCING TRUE HAPPINESS.

Be Free!

19

PROTECTED FROM THE POISON

Leave the drama behind you. All of the nasty and horrible things that took place in your past have no place in your new life. You have been blessed to start over. You have been given a fresh start. Do not contaminate your new blessing by allowing the poison of your past to destroy the potential of your blessed future.

20

JEHOVAH RAPHA

There is nothing our God cannot do. Do not think for one moment that your past pain will cause you to miss out on the great rewards of life. Some people say, "I'll never be able heal from old hurts!" This is a lie. There is no burden, no breakup, no divorce, no abuse or anything agonizing that God cannot flip into a positive. He will do it just for you. Before you commit to a relationship make sure God has totally healed you.

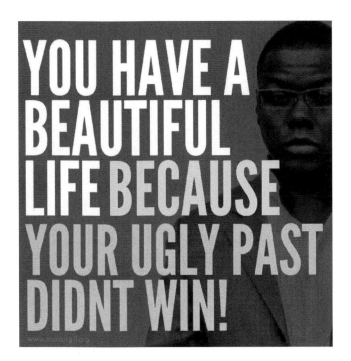

21

THE PAST HAS NO POWER!

We all have a past. There is something about all of us that we really do not want anyone to know about. Being completely honest, we would all have to admit that we wish we could reverse some things that we have done in our past. We have made decisions at some point in time during our life's journey that should have landed us in the worst of punishment. Furthermore, there are some decisions that we have made that should have resulted in our own death. I am sure that you and I have many reasons to rejoice and give God our greatest praise, simply because He covered us. Though our past was ugly, God gave us chance after chance to be beautiful all over again. There are many reasons for this.

This section of the book may not be for everybody. There are folks who would rather not admit that they have ever made a mistake in their life. For those of us who are willing to admit it, we can appreciate our past in a greater way. We know that God has brought us from a mighty long way! Praise God!

My personal testimony is admittedly ugly. When I look back on the foolish things in which I purposely participated, I almost want to hide my face. The choices that I once made should have left me in a place of eternal misery. There were times where I felt like my decisions were so bad that God had lifted His anointing off of my life and left me to my own degenerate mind. I remember praying to God, not even sure that He would even hear my prayer. I told God that if He would give me a way of escape from my place of torment, I would give Him my whole heart, mind, body and soul, for the work of building His Kingdom. I rejoice today because He heard my prayer.

When I make mention of your life being beautiful, I am giving you a visual description of who you are now, because you made it through the worst season of your life. There are so many people who have been through the same struggles that you have been through and they did not make it. Some have committed suicide because they could not handle the consequences of their own decisions. Mental institutions are filled with great people who just simply lost their minds because of the results of their bad choices. This is not your outcome. You have been blessed and favored of God to have no sign of destruction. The mistakes that you've made in the past only prepared you for a non-cycled sin life.

Sadly, our worst past choices came under the influence of somebody else. Although family and friends can be a bad influence at times, our hardest falls come from romantic relationship connections. We get so attached to someone that we forget all about our morals. We allow our flesh to think and make decisions for us. Knowing that the spirit of God is our guide, most of us ignore His still small voice because we want to do what we want to do. The worst choice we ever made was to ignore the voice of God. Thank God for his beautiful grace. Our ugly past taught us a great lesson. Anybody with good sense, like you, does not want to repeat the ugly past. The only experience to have now is a beautiful present and future.

God has His hand on you. The destination that God has already set up for your life could not be left empty. Grace and mercy spared our lives so that we could walk in the fullness of God's glory. You are preparing for the most amazing life. You are still alive and in your right mind. You must be grateful for the bad, it has worked for your good!

Bible Reference:

Ephesians 2:8 For by grace you are saved through faith, and this is not from yourselves, it is the gift of God;

YOUR GOD SENT MATE WILL HATE ARGUING. CONFLICT WILL BE RESOLVED PEACEFULLY.

22

ARGUE FOR WHAT?

Conflict is not always avoidable. We would all love to live in a world where there is the existence of peace all of the time. The dream to wake up every day and be at peace about everything seems to remain just that, a dream. When it comes to our relations with people, for those of us who really walk by faith with the love of the Lord, we want our relationships with people to be nothing less than everlasting joy. Does this always happen? No. In fact, the people that we are the closest to at times are the people who cause the most trouble in our lives. Thank God there is never any love lost. The greatest idea is to meet someone who is totally conflict free. We always pray, "Lord, please allow the mate that you send me to be drama free, amen!" I really believe that God hears our prayers and is ready to give us just that. This answered prayer does not come in a perfect package. There will be times of trouble. There will be times of disagreement. The difference between a random person and your God-sent mate is that the person who God sends you will not enjoy arguing. Does this mean arguments will never happen? No. It does mean it will not be intentional. Thank God in advance for that.

There are some people who are so angry with their own life that the only pleasure they get out of life is seeing someone else miserable. Often times, the best single people commit to relationships with people like this. This negative personality trait stays hidden for quite a while. When you get into the swing of things with this type of person, they already know that you are a happier persona than they are. They will act as if they are in celebration with you for a while. Soon afterwards the acting stops. It is only because of jealously that these type of individuals will begin to "raise hell" in your relationship. Understand this: When you have the joy of the Lord in your heart, there are times where you can be perceived to be too happy. Negative, jealous, and/or miserable people cannot stand that. They will be willing to commit to a relationship with you because they want what you have, but they do not realize that an emotion so strong needs to be delivered from them before committing to a relationship. This is why they will fight you so much. They know you are a peaceful person. They know arguing disturbs your happiness. People with this attitude will purposefully start arguments with you. Things that are not even a big deal they will make into the biggest deal. The will purposely make plans to avoid making commitments to support you. They will spend money that you both agreed to save. They will avoid doing the things that you have peacefully asked of them to do, just to cause conflict on purpose. I have been there. I have experienced it. I asking of small and honorable favors. With no reason in the world to say no, you get a no response just because the opposite party knows that a yes will make you happy. They don't want to see you happy because they are jealous. This is when you know for sure you are not with your God-sent mate; this is someone you chose alone.

The person who God sends will already be healed. The same joy that you bask in on a daily basis, will be the same joy that they have. When conflict does arise (and it will not be often), you both will find the most peaceable ways to resolve it. You will support each other with no reservations. You will make each other smile. You both will be able to respectfully converse and make decisions together. Your God-sent mate will know how to respect you for who you are and you will know the same for them. Your relationship will be one of peace and "verbal-fight free".

Bible Reference:

Philippians 2:14-16 Do everything without grumbling or arguing, so that you may be blameless and pure, children of God without blemish though you live in a crooked and perverse society, in which you shine as lights in the world, by holding on to the word of life so that on the day of Christ I will have a reason to boast that I did not run in vain nor labor in vain.

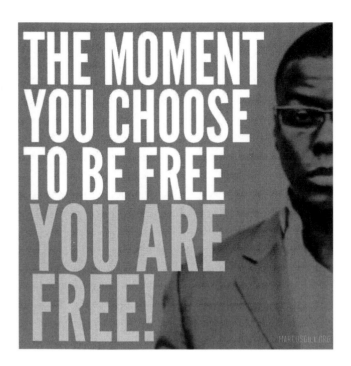

23

YOU HAVE THE KEY.

The worst thing that any individual can do is expect the worst. Most of us have been in a relationship at some point and time that we wish would could go back in time and avoid it. The pain form the relationships that we have been in seems to never leave. Outside of the moments when we use our testimony to inspire someone else, we think about our past and the thoughts associated with it are ugly. When it comes to our relationship life, we find ourselves holding onto the former experience.

This is a big problem. When we hold on to past experiences, expecting them to repeat themselves, we can block out present and future blessings.

I truly believe that in every experience there is a lesson to be learned. God allows some things to happen to teach us a quick lesson, but then we move on. We are not supposed to be bound by the negative experiences that we have had in life and relationships. Most good men and good women get into a committed relationship, get treated like trash, and then never want to commit to anyone again. Why? The person that treated them like trash could not fully appreciate their good because they have not been freed from the previous hurt that they had. This happens over and over again, and now you just have a lot of good people who are still bound by old experiences. You just may be one of them. You do not have to stay one.

The moment that you decide to be free, you are free. You have to really get it in your heart, mind and spirit that you refuse to miss out on what God has planned for your future. People who are not free from past bad experiences build invisible walls. They will not speak to people. They will not be friends with people. They will not exchange even a giggle because they are afraid of a repeat failure. Some women think that all men are dogs. Some men think that all women are scammers. This is because of one or even a few past hurts from their previous relationships. All men and women are not just like your ex.

God is so amazing in all of His ways. He is so large, that there is no way that we could ever put Him in a box and suggest that all of His own creations are the same. You must believe by faith that there is someone out there waiting and looking for you, who will never be like your past failures. I know deep down inside you really believe this; but, in order for you to have it, you have to be free from your past bondage. You have to be determined to know the truth about who you are first. Stop living your life and making decisions based upon how someone else treated you. I will use my own testimony of how my past experience was not the best at all. Furthermore, I do know that I was a good man. I do know that not everyone will know how to treat a good man like me. I also know that if I do not let go of the pain from my past, I will miss out on the pleasure of my future. I myself had to get free, free in my mind and heart. I had to forgive and move forward. Know this: the rest of your life is longer than your past. Do not hold on to a painful temporary moment and miss out on everlasting joy.

I love God. He has someone waiting or looking for you who is already free. In this next phase of your relationship life, you will not have to fight and survive someone else's punishment. Prayerfully, your God-sent mate will not be punished by you either. Right now, as you are reading this section, begin to declare your freedom! You hold the key to your joy. Use it, unlock the door of your heart and mind, forgive them, and be free to enjoy your new life!

Bible Reference:

1 Peter 2:16 Live as people who are free, not using your freedom as a cover-up for evil, but living as servants of God.

WHEN GOD SAYS NO DONT IGNORE HIM HE KNOWS WHAT YOU DONT KNOW YOU WILL REJOICE LATER.✓

24

NO MEANS NO.

God knows all. God knew what you were going to go through before you went through it. God knew what your right now would look like before you arrived at it today. More importantly, God knows your future before you walk into it. We trust and believe in God. We have faith in God. We know and believe that God is omniscient, which means He is all-knowing. We also know that God has all of the answers to our life's questions. He knows what you need to be perfectly happy and successful in your next relationship. We love God and we know God has our best, but do we always desire to accept His plan?

Truth be told, we want to do life the way we want to do it. We pray and ask God to bless us, heal us, and guide us; but when He does, we do not always listen. God does not always agree with our prayers. God will answer our prayers in three different ways. Sometimes God will say yes, sometimes "no" and sometimes "wait". As firm believers in God, we must be willing to accept whatever His answer is at all times. Even when God's answer does not match our request, we must still rejoice because God's answer is always the best answer. God makes no mistakes. We do. Our biggest mistake in life concerning any prayer request sent to God is to ignore God's answer. Do not do it.

As you are preparing for your God-sent mate, you must realize that God is going to speak to you. God is not going to control you and literally make decisions for you. What God does is so unique. He will allow us to make our own decisions. However, God will also speak to us to lead us and guide us in the right direction. It is our responsibility to hear, recognize, and be obedient to the voice of God. Even when the answer that God gives does not match up with our own desires, if we are willing to obey his commands, we will rejoice in the end. You must remember. God can always see better than what you can see. You cannot confuse the two.

I reflect on some of the relationship choices that I have made and I get shaken. I am shaken because I can remember hearing the voice of the almighty God telling me, "No!" See, the voice that God uses when He speaks to us is not always audible. Most of the time, God's voice comes through perspicacity. God will allow us to see things that would normally be hidden. That is called your gift of discernment. When those things that you pray and ask God to keep out of your life keep showing up through your potential mate, that is God's way of saying "no". The fact that you can see exactly what it is that you do not want is a clear sign that a particular individual is not the one for you. I warn you not to ignore the voice of God. When we do, we set ourselves up for a long period or even a lifetime of misery. I can remember knowing things that I purposely wanted to avoid. I was able to see personality traits that I hated, yet I ignored them because I thought I was strong enough and able enough to change them. I knew that God was using those visuals as a way of saying, "Marcus, no!" The misery comes when we have to endure our painful experience because we did not listen to God. The rejoicing comes when you listen to the voice of God and you step away and then you realize why God was saying no in the first place.

The worst thing for you to do is ignore the voice of God when it pertains to choosing your mate. You must be willing and obedient to follow God's instructions. When you see the very opposite of what you desire, do not settle. God is allowing you to see clearly before you commit to the wrong one.

Bible Reference:

1 Corinthians 2:10-11 For to us God revealed them through the Spirit; for the Spirit searches all things, even the depths of God. For who among men knows the thoughts of a man except the spirit of the man which is in him? Even so the thoughts of God no one knows except the Spirit of God.

DONT MAKE THE MISTAKE OF FALLING IN LOVE WITH THEIR MASK.

25

GOOD ACTING

God is the creator of all things. Everything that God makes is real. He makes no fakes. Nothing that God does is ever phony. There is no character trait in God that could display a lie. He cannot lie. I believe that one of the things that God hates the most is lying. So believe me, God does not want His very own children to be fooled by lies. You are one of His children, and you deserve to fall in love with a real person and not their mask.

Too many times great people commit to relationships based upon the good acting of the opposite partner. Unfortunately, people feel as if they must change who they really are in order to make it in life. Even worse, people will do anything in the world to impress a man or a woman just to get them to commit to a relationship. This negative behavior is not of God. You may be in a current situation where you are giving your all. You are giving your mate or potential mate the authentic you. In every conversation, you are being totally honest, you never hide your feelings or opinions. Perhaps you have even been totally honest about your past experiences in life whether they be good or bad. You share your weaknesses and your failures. In other words, you have been absolutely transparent in revealing who you are to this person. This is a good thing. Some people would say that it is not good to reveal so much truth about yourself so early, but I disagree. I feel as though one should be totally transparent in the beginning, because whatever you hide will eventually come out in the long run. If you keep it real from the start, you give the opposite party a real opportunity to make a real decision about being with you. The sad thing about this is, you never know if your potential mate is being just as honest as you are. This is another reason for praying and asking God to show you things beyond what you can see in the natural.

Masks look really good. Only in a play or scary movie will you see a mask that has the purpose of scaring you away. In life, people wear masks to cover up reality. They wear masks to draw people to them. If you ever see someone who would possibly be wearing a mask and they are evil, chances are they are not wearing a mask, that is the real them. Funny to mention, these people are better to deal with than those who want to cover up their true selves. I would rather fall in love with someone who is not so good and honest about it, than to fall in love with someone who is being fake about their glory.

My personal testimony includes an experience of being attracted to the costume. I was fooled into seeing the way someone looks on the outside and not really knowing who they were on the inside. The speech was everything that I wanted to hear. The clothes that were worn before me were the perfect example of what I wanted my significant other to look like. The gifts and abilities to be a firm ministry partner were on display. The costume of a loving, humble, God-fearing woman, was being worn before me and all of the important people in my life. All I could see were my dreams coming true. When I tell you that I was in love with what I thought was the answer to my prayers, I am telling the whole truth. The mask was being worn well. I fell for the outward actions and appearance that was designed to trick me into commitment. As a mask is worn for performing arts, the real person is covered by who they want the audience to see and believe. The real person is revealed backstage after the show is over. Well, in my life, the show lasted and the show ended. The real person had to eventually be revealed. I was highly disappointed. It is one of the worst feelings in the world.

Know this: If your potential mate is wearing a mask and performing well, the show does not last forever. Eventually, they will get tired of faking things. Even worse, they will run out of space to hide their true self. People cannot hide forever. We must pray and ask God to help us to see in advance. The outward appearance of a man or woman can be very appealing, but it is the inside of a person that cannot be faked. Do not be fooled. Your God-sent mate will not wear a mask. They will not put on a good show just to impress you, your family, or friends. They will be real with you. The man or woman that decides to be transparent with their potential mate is always on God's side of doing things.

I also encourage you to avoid wearing a mask yourself. God made you wonderfully. You have a plethora of great characteristics and I am sure you have a few flaws, but realize this: You are still an amazing person. God has blessed you with an overflow of greatness. You do not have to wear a mask or a costume. You must be you. If you ever so happen to be fooled by the mask of the opposite party, please know that as long as your intentions are right, God will create a way of escape for you and give you another chance to take your time and hear from Him the next time you decide to date. I declare over your life that you will not be fooled by a mask or false representative of your potential mate.

Bible Reference:

2 Timothy 3:5 - Having a form of godliness, but denying the power thereof: from such turn away.

YOUR FUTURE
MATE WILL HELP BRING
OUT THE BEST
OF GODS GIFT IN YOU.
NOT SEPARATE YOU FROM
YOUR GOD GIVEN
ASSIGNMENT.

26

YOU MUST REFUSE TO BE DETACHED!

You are called and chosen to do great things for the Lord. The will of God being done in your life should be your number one priority. As you are preparing for your God-sent mate, you must know that God will send you someone who is excited about helping you fulfill your God-given assignment. If you ever realize that you're dating someone who is a distraction from your spiritual tasks, know that they are not sent by God.

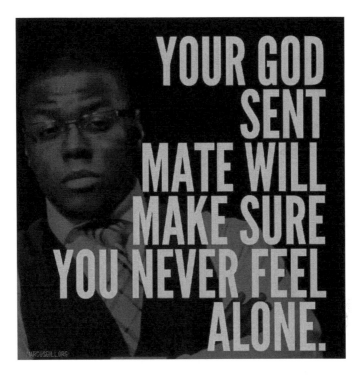

YOUR GOD SENT MATE WILL MAKE SURE YOU NEVER FEEL ALONE.

MARCUSGILL.ORG

27

NEVER ALONE

God is going to bless you with someone who will make sure that every moment of your life is filled with as much joy as they can deliver. Even those moments when they cannot be with you physically, they will make sure that you know that you are on their mind. Random phone calls, loving text messages, cards that express how much they really love you, will come to you often. When God sends the one, you will never be left wondering.

IM WAITING

IM NOT WORRYING BECAUSE
I KNOW GOD IS WORKING ON
SOMETHING AMAZING
JUST FOR ME.

28

AN AMAZING DELIVERY IS COMING SOON!

When you truly believe God, you know that your waiting is not a waste of time. God has a special blessing just for you. As you are in your waiting season, do not worry but instead worship! Know that there is a blessing in waiting on God. Worship in advance for the amazing blessing (person) that God has just for you! Let your waiting be filled with excitement!

29

NO COMPETITION

One of the worst experiences in relationships that I have ever had was being with someone who was jealous of me. This type of jealously is one that occurs when you both have the same God- given ability and one of you happens to be in a greater place than the other. If you do not identify this negative spirit early, you will always be miserable trying to work as a team. They will try to secretly keep you down. Watch out.

know this
YOUR GOD SENT MATE WILL MAKE YOU SHINE! NOT DESTROY YOUR LIGHT BECAUSE OF INSECURITY AND JEALOUSLY.

www.marcusgill.org

30

GOD WILL SEND YOU A GREAT TEAM-MATE.

The greatest answer to an anointed single person's prayer is when God sends someone into their life who helps them to move forward. A couple that knows that they both make each other shine will make the best power team. This is impossible to have when the other mate is jealous or insecure about their role in the relationship. Your God sent mate will be glad to see you shine. They will know that when one shines, you both shine!

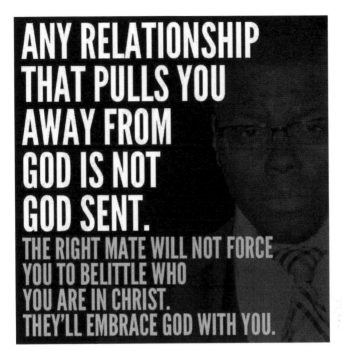

ANY RELATIONSHIP THAT PULLS YOU AWAY FROM GOD IS NOT GOD SENT. THE RIGHT MATE WILL NOT FORCE YOU TO BELITTLE WHO YOU ARE IN CHRIST. THEY'LL EMBRACE GOD WITH YOU.

31

EMBRACE MY GOD.

One of the worst experiences as a child of God is to connect with people who do not love, honor, and respect the God you serve. One thing that I know that Satan loves to see is a focused and dedicated child of God lose focus. These distractions that come into our life are not always designed to pull us away from work or family; these distractions come ultimately to destroy our focus and relationship with God. What greater way does the enemy use to throw us off course, than to use our hearts? Every so often, you hear the testimony of an individual who meets a wonderful and charming person. They are on fire for God and then over time you begin to see them back away from the things of God. They do not come to church as often because they are on dates. They do not pray as often because they are spending more time on the phone with their mate. Suddenly, this awesome praise and worship leader, prayer warrior, evangelist, or preacher is not so active in ministry anymore. What happened? They ended up with a boyfriend or girlfriend, and all of their focus and attention leaves the work of God and points to the relationship. Not always, but most often, this happened when an individual who is on fire for God ends up dating a person who really does not serve the Lord like them. Therefore, this person gets pulled away from the things of God. Before they even realize it, they have totally been pulled away from their once dedicated life to God.

You may not be a high ranking ministry official, but you may have a great relationship with God. You love the Lord with all of your heart. You worship and pray daily. You engage in conversations that bring glory to God. You are focused. You have a great life. You know how to have fun outside of spiritual things, yet you know how to balance your life so that you never disrespect God. As you are dating and seeking God for the mate that He will send you, please know this: God will not send you someone who will be a distraction to your walk with Him. Sometimes, we can get so caught up into the other individual and not even realize that we are slowing drifting away. Do not let this happen to you.

Here is an unhappy reality. Sometimes, these mates are also church attendees. You can meet someone who is in church and just as into God as you are. Yet, they may not be as close to God as you are. There are so many hypocrites in the church. These are the people who know how to fake the funk! They know how to wear the church mask really well. You can end up dating one of these types of people. Even though they are in the church just as much as you are, they may not be as strong and focused on a real personal relationship with God like you. So at the same time, you must not be so quick to fall into a relationship with a person just because they are in church. You must find out their level of relationship with God. Just as fast as someone who is unsaved can draw your focus and attention away from God, the same can happen by the influence of a fellow church-goer.

Your God-sent mate will love God just like you, if not deeper. The person that you are believing God for should be the type of person who draws you closer to God and not away from Him. They will encourage personal prayer, fasting, and worship. Your God- sent mate will not allow you to fall short of the glory of God. They will respect your relationship with God. The days and nights that you have scheduled to attend church services they will purposely plan around them to respect your devotion to God. They will never force you to do things that world suggests for fun, especially if it causes you to disappoint God. They will honor your walk. Even if they are not as strong in the Lord as you, they will admire your devotion to God and have a desire to join you. Furthermore, your God-sent mate will celebrate your growth in Christ. They will not make jokes of your walk with God. They must be willing and ready to magnify God with you and fully embrace your ability to stay before the Lord.

Bible Reference:

1 Corinthians 6:9 Know ye not that the unrighteous shall not inherit the kingdom of God? Be not deceived: neither fornicators, nor idolaters, nor adulterers, nor effeminate, nor abusers of themselves with mankind,

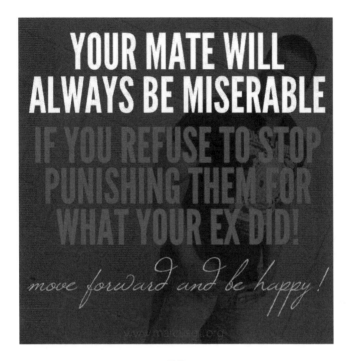

YOUR MATE WILL ALWAYS BE MISERABLE IF YOU REFUSE TO STOP PUNISHING THEM FOR WHAT YOUR EX DID!

move forward and be happy!

32

YOUR EX IS GONE.

As you plan to move forward, you must be willing to let go of the past. There is no way that you are ever going to be fully happy and experience the real joy of love if you hold on to old stuff. Though this book has been full of warnings about how to avoid the negative attacks that come against good people like you, I must encourage you not to be the trouble.

You may have been through some of the worst relationships. I certainly have. I also know in my heart that the best thing to do in order for us to truly enjoy the God-sent mate that God has for us is to go of the old hurt. The past is over. Every so often, we do have flash backs. We look back sometimes and feel a bit of pain because of the horrible things that we have been through; yet, we have no excuse to punish our God-sent mate for the things that were done to us in the past. We must move on and move forward. We must take those experiences and make sure that they build us up to really appreciate the blessing that God has for us in the near future.

As I reflect on some of the experiences of my past negative relationships, I can testify about being on the other end of the stick. I know for a fact that I was a genuinely good man. I am in no way saying that I was perfect, but one thing I do know is that I did not deserve the punishment that I received without warning. Can you imagine getting fussed out for things that someone else did? I was saying to myself, "I do not even know these people!" You find yourself doing all that you can to prove yourself worthy of trust, respect, and love; yet, you get blatant disrespect and misdirected punishment. It makes no sense. The pain of knowing that that all of your positive and well thought out attempts to put a smile on your mate's face is all in vain is heartbreaking. I tell you from experience that treating a good person horribly because of your fears that were created because of your past will cause them to leave you.

Unfortunately, this is a part of my testimony. I have had to walk away from a few relationships simply because of the frustration of trying to constantly prove myself to be real. Please do not lose the great individual that God sends into your life by treating them like a criminal. You want your God-sent mate to be full of joy and not miserable. They will be absolutely miserable if you find yourself punishing them for what your EX did. Your EX is out of the picture. I am sure at some point you found yourself praying and asking God to deliver you from that bad relationship and He did it. It would be a slap in God's face for you to continue to live in that pain after He delivers you. You have been blessed with freedom. Am I saying that it was not painful? No. I will say that that pain came with a purpose. The only reason you should look back should be to see where God has brought you from.

In this season of your life, I encourage you to be free and move forward. God has blessed you with a fresh start, a brand new life. The Word of God tells us that if anyone be in Christ, they are a new creature. Old things have passed away and behold all things have become new. Toss out the old drama and embrace your new life. God has someone ready to help you heal from the pain of your past, but you must let them do it with joy. Someone who is miserable cannot heal another miserable person. It is like the blind leading the blind. It is really sad when the God-sent person comes into your life to help heal you and you make them miserable and cause them to leave. Then, you end up adding another person to your list of people who left you.

The worst feeling that I believe one could have (and I have had this feeling before) is to look up and realize that you had the perfect mate and your own selfishness and ignorance caused them to walk away. I have good news for you: This does not have to be your story. You can make up in your mind that you refuse to hold on to dead weight. You will let go of the trash from your past and move forward with joy, peace, and freedom to embrace your blessed future!

Bible Reference:

John 8:36 So if the Son sets you free, you will be free indeed.

33

PERSONALITY COUNTS THE MOST.

When I was in college, I heard the term, "trophy woman" for the first time. This type of woman was being described to a group of young men, including myself, as a woman who looks amazing and all she is good for is standing next to you for you to show off. She did not have to be smart or respectful. All she had to do is stand on your arm so that you can sub-willingly say to everyone you brought her around, "Look at what I have". This is subconsciously the goal of a lot of guys and gals. Naturally, you want a mate that is easy to look at. You want someone who you can proudly show off before your friends and family. You want to be proud when you pull his or her picture out on your phone or photo album. Often times, the first thing that attracts two individuals is the outward appearance. "Wow he/she looks good. Hook me up!" LOL! We look first at the amazing beauty or handsomeness of the opposite sex, which is not a bad thing. It is actually a great thing. However, the only mistake that comes with that is the inability to read a person's true character because we are so caught up on how good they look. There is no problem with appreciating their good looks. Yet, you are going to have a huge problem if you ignore their ugly personality.

The truth of the matter is everybody has some type of beauty. I always tell people that I have never met an ugly person. Beauty is in the eye of the beholder. This in one of the truest statements ever made. Unfortunately, the eye does not always recognize personality at first sight. It takes time to get to know someone deeply. As God fearing people, we must be mature enough to look beyond someone's outward appearance. Not to say that you must avoid people who are attractive to your eyes, but you must also know that outward looks are not more important than a person's inner man. This is one of the biggest mistakes that men and women make while dating someone who they think will be their potential mate. They get so caught up in their glamourous looks and they purposely ignore the faulty personality traits of the opposite individual. Why? Because the looks become more important than their happiness. Do not make this mistake.

There have been times in my life where I claimed to have a trophy mate. I claimed such not only because of the looks, but because she had stunning looks, amazing talents, and gifts, and was anointed to serve in ministry; and in my eyes, we made a great team. All of these things were what I thought automatically made a great mate. I saw the female version of myself, but eventually I began to feel the pain of the personality traits that I ignored in the beginning. If your potential mate is negative, you will not be impressed with their good looks once their negative personality traits begin to be revealed. Furthermore, in some cases, the negative character of an individual is revealed early; but once again, they look so amazing that you ignore it only for those looks to wear off after a few months of commitment. Sadly, that personality of a person will always exist. Do not be blind!

I have learned to appreciate the opposite individual who does not focus more on their own appearance than they do their intellect. The looks of a person will either get better naturally or fade away naturally, especially those who decide to pay for the enhancing of their looks. This includes you. Know who you are. Know that you are amazingly stunning inside and out. Do not be the trophy that someone is looking for, only to carry you around, show you off, and then get home and ignore you because they really do not like you for you. A very funny thought is one of getting to know this beautiful person and finding out how ignorant they are and then their looks are not even appealing anymore. When at one time you refused to take your eyes off of them, now you cannot stand to see them or hear their voice.

Whatever you do, do not get stuck in a horrible relationship because you chose to dwell on appearance and not personality.

Bible Reference:

2 Timothy 3:13 But evil men and seducers shall wax worse and worse, deceiving, and being deceived.

Is not a status. It's word that describes a person who is strong enough to enjoy life alone while waiting on GOD'S BEST

34

SINGLE AND STRONG

I would never be able to count the amount of times that I have been asked this most famous question, "Are you single?" Before and even after my divorce, I would often answer by saying, "Yes, I am single." Then, God began to reveal better answers. I will share those answer options with you at the end of this section.

People, often times we see someone who is alone and think they are sad. I used to do it all of the time.

If I happened to be out to eat or in the mall and see someone sitting alone, eating alone, or shopping alone, the assumption would be that they were miserable or depressed. Sometimes, you may have done it too. We will quickly begin to feel sorry for them just because they are alone at the moment. Without even knowing, we start judging them. They may be happily married with children. They may be waiting for a loving mate to meet them there. However, just as we have assumed, they may even actually be single. Most of the time they are. I have been out to eat, to the movies, to sporting events, to church, and many others public places, alone. Some of my friends oftentimes ask me, "Aren't you bored? Aren't you lonely? Don't you feel weak being alone?" I always answer with a confident, "No." I have learned how to enjoy me.

I believe that single is not a status. It is a word that describes a person who is strong enough to enjoy life alone while waiting on God's best. The truth of the matter is you must be a strong person these days anyway. Let alone being alone, you have really got to be strong. You must be able to stand on your own two feet. Even though having a significant other is a great thing, you must be able to understand that standing alone can be a great thing too. When you can enjoy life alone, you can be happy at any time. There are some people who feel as if they cannot enjoy their life with the benefit of someone to enjoy it with. That is not so horrible, but it does not display strength. If you are in the place of waiting on God to reveal to you your future mate, you have to stand strong alone.

People who are in need of a partner to enjoy life with will rush into a relationship with anybody. That is weakness. When you cannot experience the bliss of life alone, you really do not need to try it with anyone else because it is obvious that you do not already appreciate yourself. This does not mean for you to expect to be alone forever. I am not giving you this word to cause you to lose your desire to be with someone. I want you to wait patiently on your God-sent mate. Furthermore, I want you to be able to enjoy your life while waiting.

You certainly deserve God's best and nothing less. You have to know first that you will be someone else's best one day. You have to have your own confidence stirred up, not arrogance but confidence. Yet, be humble enough to share your happiness and joy with the one that God sends you. Once upon a time, I was in that weak place. I felt as if I would not be able to fulfill the calling on my life for ministry without a mate. I did not know how to enjoy my life alone, so I ended up rushing into a relationship. It was the wrong relationship to commit to. How did I end up in this place? One of the reasons was because I did not love myself enough to patiently wait on

God's best. So, I ended up choosing what I thought to be my best and I failed.

A good way for a strong individual like yourself to respond to the famous, "Are you single?" question, would be to answer with, "I am just enjoying waiting on God". Our bible tells us that patience is a virtue. Virtue is defined a good and moral quality. Do you have the power and moral quality to wait on God's best? Are you strong enough to enjoy your life while being single? If so, you better prepare yourself for an awesome testimony of God's relationship making power.

Bible Reference:

Lamentations 3:25 The LORD is good to those who wait for him, to the soul who seeks him.

35

SPIRIT OVER FLESH

The power of God is so awesome. One thing that I love about our God is that He surely takes care of His own children. He will lead us and guide us through our entire life. God makes sure that that our walk with Him has the chance to be flawless. I truly believe that God never wants to see His own children fail. I know this because He provides for us resources that we should follow daily to be sure that we stay on track to His way of doing things. We have the bible, the written word of God. We also have His unique and still small voice that speaks to us. See, it is never God who fails us. It is us who fail God at times. The greatest part about our God is, even when we fail, He still loves us and forgives us. We must do our best job to honor His hand of love in our lives.

As we are in preparation to make a commitment to that special person that God has waiting for us to be ready, we must learn to recognize the voice of God. Now, the voice of God does not come audibly out of the sky, but He speaks to us through our spirit. The way you hear the voice of God may be different from the way that I hear the voice of God. He may speak to you though others, or perhaps in dreams, even through what you see. One thing is for sure: when you have a true relationship with God, you are able to recognize His voice in any form in which He comes. The only mistake that we make at times is ignoring His subtle warnings. This is when we fail because we allow our flesh to override what God is trying to reveal. We may have temporary satisfaction doing this, but in the long run, it will all catch up to us and it is never an appealing experience.

Our flesh wants what it wants. Normally our flesh will hunger and thirst for the petty things of this world, the things that are made for temporary pleasure. Know this: our flesh is already temporary. It will not last forever. Our flesh will one day die. This is why fleshy things do not hold any validation in our spiritual lives because it will only exist for just a moment. Spiritual things are the things that are eternal. Even though our relationships are made for our experience here on earth, we must allow the spirit of God to guide us in all things concerning this because He honors marriage.

Here is one of the greatest examples of allowing your flesh to win over your spirit. When sex before marriage takes place, it goes against God's plan. Therefore, you end up having more turmoil than peace. You have allowed your flesh to override what you know to be true of the spirit. How often do we all do this? I have had so many downfalls in my past because I refused to allow God's word to be my guide in life, especially concerning relationships.

The Holy Spirit will reveal things to you. Often times, it is the things that we do not want to hear that our spirit makes us aware of aka the truth or the reality of the relationship. Your spirit will say no when your flesh is saying yes. Do not let your flesh cover what the spirit is trying to reveal. Your flesh is not the guide. Your flesh is not the winner. Your spirit is your guide. You must allow the spirit in you to guide your decision making. My prayer has been that my heart's desire would be to only desire what God wants for me and my life. Too often, the enemy and his demons lay distractions before our eyes. Good looks, sex, money, fame and so many more things all look good to our natural eyes. Remember, these things are just temporary and they will fade away. You will be lost forever if you make a relationship decision based upon your flesh being pleased. God will be warning you. Your inner spirit man will be screaming at you to turn the other way. Do not get fooled or tricked into making a commitment because of momentary pleasures.

The spirit of God speaks to you to protect you, not to harm you or make your life as a Christian boring. It is better to deny your flesh from a temporary experience, and embrace the spirit of the Lord that will lead you into eternal joy. You can win the fight!

Bible Reference:

Daniel 2:22 It is He who reveals the profound and hidden things; He knows what is in the darkness, and the light dwells with Him.

ABSTINENCE PROTECTS YOUR MIND -BODY - SOUL AND SPIRIT.

MARCUSGILL.ORG

36

TRUE LOVE WAITS.

Yes it may sound old school, but it is the truth. When you have sex with someone because you think they are your potential mate, you ruin everything! My own personal testimony is the proof behind why I believe in this statement. You move too fast out of God's will. You yield your mind, body, soul and spirit when you give them the benefit of sex. This is why you end up lost and controlled by them so quickly. Do not give it up!

37

SHORT TERM JOY FOR LONG TERM TROUBLE

So, I randomly used twenty-nine minutes to paint a picture. I am sure you get it. It is no time compared to the amount of minutes left in the rest of your life. However, so many people give up everything for a brief moment of pleasure to end up being totally miserable for life. There is great pride in waiting on God. God's greatest blessings are worth more and will last a lot longer than that little moment in bed with a stranger! Yes, if you are in the bed with someone before marriage, they are not your friend. A true friend/lover will help you wait on God! They will help you avoid falling before the eyes of God. They will help you wait because they will be excited about waiting with you! Get ready for a lifetime of pleasure!

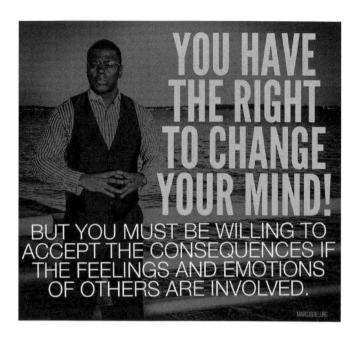

YOU HAVE THE RIGHT TO CHANGE YOUR MIND! BUT YOU MUST BE WILLING TO ACCEPT THE CONSEQUENCES IF THE FEELINGS AND EMOTIONS OF OTHERS ARE INVOLVED.

MARCUSGILL.ORG

<u>38</u>

YOU HAVE RIGHTS WITH RESPOSIBILITY.

One of the worst things someone can do to another person is to purposely play with their heart. The truth of the matter is, some people do not do this on purpose. There is such a thing as having a change of heart. The mature thing to do if this decision ever has to be made is make sure you take responsibly for how you made their heart rest in assurance that you would be there forever. Do not feel guilty, but you have a role to play in this season of waiting and searching as well. As much as you do not want your heart broken, make sure you do not break anyone else's.

39

NO JUNK

It is a brand new day for you. Make sure that you do not return to your old way of doing things. Your days of making decisions based upon what your flesh wants are over. Floating from person to person trying to find happiness is not your style. I was once in this sad place in life. Living a Godly lifestyle will help open the doors for God to pour out major blessings on your life. Your God- sent mate will not be messy either!

40

HAVE A BLAST WITH YOU!

Have a good time alone. Being single is not a problem. If fact, I would like to call it the greatest blessing before getting married. You must be able to enjoy your own space before you can share it. Stop looking down on yourself and feeling like you are only single because you are not good enough for another person. You are the best version of you that God ever created. Enjoy your own space. Make the best of your own personal time!

YOU MAY HELP THEM BUT IT DOESNT MEAN THEY LOVE YOU! GUARD YOUR HEART.

MARCUSGILL.ORG

41

HELP YOUR HEART.

We have often heard the saying, "It's just nice to be nice!" This is most certainly a true statement. For unselfish people, this type of behavior comes automatically. Knowing that we have the ability to help someone makes our own heart glad. Our Bible tells us to do unto others as we would have them do unto us. Somewhere along the line, we misinterpret that text from the Bible. We assume that that scripture means that what we do for others will automatically return to us, kind of like karma. If I am evil, mean, or selfish to others, I should expect for others to be mean, evil, or selfish to me. On the contrary, if I am loving, giving, and loyal to others, I should automatically be granted that same loving, giving, and loyal care from others. Sadly, it does not always work like that. Furthermore, the people who are the most positive to others oftentimes get the opposite treatment in return. One of the most painful experiences with this happens when you are in a committed romantic relationship.

You may be the type of person who loves hard. You give everything that you have. You will do whatever it takes to make your partner happy. Your reputation is one of being a helping, loving, giving, and unselfish person. So, when the news is out that you are single, so many want to connect with you because they certainly want the benefits of such a great person. This is not a bad thing. People are supposed to want you because of your amazing character. The only problem that you will have is when you discover that the opposite party has a hidden agenda to simply use you. Do not allow people to fake their love for you just to use you for your kindness. You have the light of God living on the inside of you. You have the God-given ability to pull someone else up. Your partner may be in a dark place, but you are gifted enough to bring them to the light. Whether it is a financial come up, emotional come up, or a spiritual uplift, you are willing, ready, and excited about being a help. It is possible to date someone who will enjoy your benefits privately, but then deep down on the inside they hate you because you are really better than them.

Sometimes, your love for people will cause you to go above and beyond without even realizing that you are being used. It is not until you look for that same level of love in return and you do not get it, that you realize that you have being giving alone. I have been there. You cannot make the assumption that your helping them guarantees their love for you.

One of the biggest mistakes that I have ever made while being in a committed relationship was assuming that my partner desired the same things that I desired. I thought in my own mind that I could help and inspire her and then be appreciated and loved for being morally good. Going above and beyond for the well-being of my partner and nothing was ever good enough. I automatically assumed if I loved her with everything I had, she would love me with everything she had. This assumption proved false! My heart was taken advantage of and I refuse to see this happen to you.

I am not encouraging you to become stingy, but I will say, do not be so quick to give everything just to help without fully evaluating the opposite person's motives. If you do not take your time, you will allow a selfish, unappreciative person to do damage to your loving heart. If you do not guard your heart, you can end up bitter. The helpful character that you have was given to you as a blessing from God. You must remain loving because your God-sent mate will actually love you and appreciate your level of help, love, and commitment. In fact, I believe God will send you someone who will try to out-love you! Your helpful heart will not go to waste. Just as I have experienced going beyond surface support for my mate and getting nothing but disrespect in return, I have the faith that one great day God would place someone in my life that would be glad to say a simple thank you. You must have faith for the same. Just do not be fooled by a user. Do not be manipulated into giving and never seeing the return. Remember that love is not automatic. Love does not come based upon how you simply treat someone. Love is real. A real person with a real heart of appreciation will love you because they are filled with the spirit of God like you are. You are blessed to be a blessing and your heart will be honored.

Bible Reference:

Proverbs 4:23 Guard your heart with all vigilance, for from it are the sources of life.

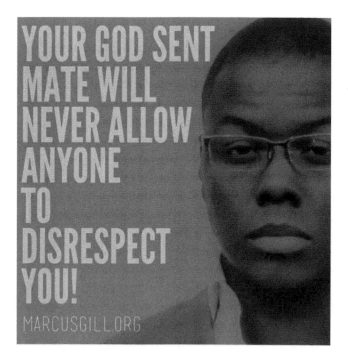

YOUR GOD SENT MATE WILL NEVER ALLOW ANYONE TO DISRESPECT YOU!

MARCUSGILL.ORG

42

NO DISRESPECT

I hate being embarrassed. Furthermore, I hate to feel embarrassed and alone at the same time. At least if I am having an embarrassing moment, let me have a chance to endure it with someone who is certainly on my team. Not all embarrassing moments happen in the same way. To slip and fall in front of a crowd, or to forget the words to a song while performing, or even walking around all day thinking that you look nice only to find out that there was a mud stain on your back all day are awkward moments. Even worse are those moments when you are left to defend yourself amongst a group of people and your mate takes sides with them. This is horrible, especially when people begin to disrespect you. Who is agreeing with you? Who is on your side? Who is supposed to be on your side? Even if you are dead wrong, shouldn't your mate at least defend you to some extent, just for loyalty purposes? Your God-sent mate will never allow anyone to disrespect you, even when you are wrong.

If you are ever dating a person who loves to disagree with you, please know that you have a big problem. One of the most obvious signs that a person is not on the same page with you is when they can never agree with you. You can make this observation in the simplest conversations. As Christians, we should only connect with someone that sees and interprets the word of God like we do. Even in those serious conversations about the word of God, when you realize that they are not on the same page with you, let that serve as a red flag as well. If they disagree with you and disrespect you privately, there are high chances that they will disagree with and disrespect you publically.

I have had a very bad experience with this. I unfortunately ignored the many obvious disagreements and disrespect that took place in private. The private disrespect in disagreeable conversations then went public. One would say, "How does this happen?" Let me give you an example. You decide to go out to eat with your mate. You make plans for your mate's family and friends to come and join you. As everyone is having a wonderful conversation about great things, some way or another, the subject matter of a previous conversation that you both had in private comes up. Now, a mature person will not seek the opinions of others, let alone, tell them that you guys had an argument about it previously. The discussion rolls on and it so happens to be that the people at the table agree with your mate's point of view. That is no big deal. However, when everyone at the table begins to bully you over your view points and your mate joins their team of bashing and slandering you, you have a big problem. Your mate has allowed others to disrespect you. When things like this happen, there is a deeper, beyond the surface reason why they would allow this to happen. They do not respect you and they are excited about seeing you jammed up because deep down on the inside they are jealous of you.

I would never allow anyone to disrespect someone that I love, especially my mate. Even if I did not agree with a view point or perspective, my loyalty would not allow me to ever embarrass my mate or ever make her feel alone. If there was ever a problem or disagreement, I would deal with it privately. You cannot ignore these subtle signs that come early during courtship.

Your God-sent mate will always defend you. They will support you. They will never take sides with others who go against you. A loyal mate will say, "I know you are dead wrong, but I am not going to leave you to hang by yourself". They will stand up for you. They will not allow people from your past to distract you from your peace. Even more so, they will defend your name and character when you are not even around. Let us go even deeper to close this section. If your mate really loves you, check this out. A true sign of their loyalty would be to cut people off who mean you no good, even if they were friends before you both met.

Bible Reference:

1 Corinthians 15:33 Do not be deceived: "Bad company ruins good morals."

RESPECT YOUR FRIENDS WHO KEEP YOU FOCUSED ON GOD!

43

RIGHT FRIENDS

As much as we think we can handle things on our own, we still need a few people in our corner to help guide us at times. We are highly intelligent and we supposedly know what we want out of a relationship; but, there are times when we must admit, we make the wrong decisions. We got what we thought we wanted and we found out that it was not what we really wanted or needed. If we take time to reflect on some of these times in our lives, we would also have to admit that there was at least one person in our life that really warned us about the bad decision we were about to make. Sadly, oftentimes when a person has a close friend who is also close to God, they ignore their advice. Moreover, the friend who gives the Godly advice get the stiff arm because they give guidance against what one's flesh wants to do. Sometimes, really good friendships are destroyed because the friend who needs the advice against what they want to do gets angry at the friend who is trying to keep them close to God. In this season of your life, you are searching for answers; you are awaiting your time of connection with your future God-sent mate. Do not lose connection with your true friends. They will help to keep you focused on the things of God and not the things of your flesh.

Respect your friends who keep you focused on God. I can remember some very painful moments in my life when I had been played by a few ladies and even where I was forced to walk away. My best friend and brother Tiont was very instrumental in making sure that I stopped making stupid mistakes when it came to choosing who I thought was supposed to be Mrs. Gill. Now even though he and I have a very relaxed and fun relationship, we never lost respect for each other. To have friends who are anointed of God is one of the greatest gifts to any child of God. Sometimes we do not see everything that we need to see. We need people to surround us that will be totally honest about our character. You need a friend who will tell you when you are wrong and when you are right. Someone to tell you when you look good and when you look terrible. We need friends that will tell us that the person that we are dating is the one and especially tell us when they can sense that we are making a big mistake.

Do not be the immature friend who cannot receive the truth, even when it hurts. I live by a principle whereas I would prefer for people to tell me what I do not want to hear opposed to telling me what only makes me feel good. Your real friends will not lie to you. They will not stand by and see you fail and celebrate as if you are having great success. There are so many battles that I would have never faced if I would have simply listened to the people in my life that really cared. They gave me the truth and I only thought that they were blocking or just trying to control my life. It was not control. It was protection. Your real friends will keep you focused on God and not the foolish things of the flesh. They will encourage to remain only in the will of God. Your real friends who truly love and serve the Lord like you will not help you make a relationship decision based upon the materialistic, fleshy desires that it seems like your potential mate can provide. True God-fearing friends will encourage you to recognize the spirit of God in your potential mate. They will pray and fast with you. Most importantly your true friends want to see you happy.

Respect them. Some things that your true friends will say just might make you upset. You have to be willing to accept the fact that they really love you and it is all for your good.

Bible Reference:

Psalm 1:1 Blessed is the man who walketh not in the counsel of the ungodly, nor standeth in the way of sinners, not sitteth in the seat of the scornful,

DO NOT MAKE A LIFETIME COMMITMENT TO THEM BASED ON ONE NICE DATE. TAKE YOUR TIME!

<u>44</u>

WE NEED MORE DATES.

Slow down! You have talked with them on the phone. You have exchanged Facebook messages, tweeted, and even tagged each other in all of your Instagram posts. The conversations with your close family members and best friends have been filled with high levels of joy because you are really feeling good about him or her. The big step is the meeting up. You have eagerly anticipated the first date. You both get dressed nice. You groom your appearance to that of a global superstar. You both have agreed on a nice place to dine and then go see a movie. Maybe you have decided to take a nice walk in the park. Who knows? LOL! You are a little nervous because you have been on a few first dates in the past and they did not go so well. You are praying. The moments when you pray, you are asking God to help guide you through this. You are asking God is he or she the one? Then, that special day finally arrives. All of your plans are executed throughout the night and you get back home (alone) and you realize that everything was absolutely perfect! Before you get too excited you must slow down and take into consideration that that was only a few hours and it was only the first time you have had a face to face encounter with this person. A few hours is nothing compared to the amount of hours that equal up to the rest of your life. Do not make a lifetime commitment to them based on one nice date.

I really cannot tell you exactly how many dates to go on before you choose to make a commitment to a relationship. Yet, what I will say is one date is certainly not enough and even five dates is not enough. You must take your time to date and really get to know someone before making a lifetime decision. You go to a nice restaurant and have a great conversation. That is all good, but that is only a door opening. You are not even inside yet. On a date, you do not get to see them angry. On a date, you do not get to meet their family members. We all hide a little bit on the first date. Think about the person that you may go on a date with that is wearing a full costume and you really do not know what you are getting yourself into. Sadly, you can go on the first night out and everything be good. Then, the second date could be a full experience of hell! I had had an experience where my mate's full costume came off within thirty days of dating. I was sitting there in my car so confused. "What happened?" I asked myself. My problem was, I did not allow that person enough time to reveal their true self. I took their early behavior as standard truth of their character. I was wrong. I was trapped.

The word of God tells us that patience is a virtue. This means that good results come from patience. We must learn how to give things time to develop. I would even go as far to say we have to learn how to give things time to break down. The spirit of discernment will allow you to see if a thing will develop or if it is going to breakdown. This is why it is so important that we are connected to God first even before dating. There are times where you may be invited on a date and you will decide not to even go because the Lord has already revealed to you that it is not a part of his plan for your life. That is just how amazing God is to His children. He does all He can to keep us from failing.

So do not be too excited. If the first date goes well, awesome. Just make sure that the next ten dates go well and that the meeting of his or her family and friends goes just a well a few times in a row. I would suggest you give yourself at least a forty-five day curiosity trial before committing to his other team. There is no rush. Take your time and enjoy the happy uncommitted moments. The good news is that you may be enjoying your God- sent mate and at the right time the official connection will happen. Do not let your early opinion decide for your life.

Bible Reference:

Colossians 2:8 Beware lest any man spoil you through philosophy and vain deceit, after the tradition of men, after the rudiments of the world, and not after Christ.

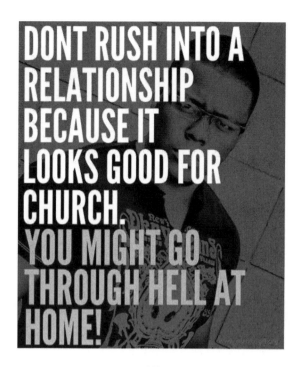

DONT RUSH INTO A RELATIONSHIP BECAUSE IT LOOKS GOOD FOR CHURCH. YOU MIGHT GO THROUGH HELL AT HOME!

45

I LIVE WITH THEM NOT YOU.

I love to encourage others. I have learned that true encouragement comes from one's personal testimony. This subject can be a very sensitive one. For someone who has been in the same position as I have been, it can be hard to live by this principle. It is only because you care. I care about the well-being of my church and ministry. So many times, I made decisions based upon what I was always taught. Most of us who grew up in strict Christian homes were taught that we should marry someone who attends the same church. Or, we must marry someone who is simply saved and filled with the Holy Spirit. Furthermore, for those of us that they knew had a call on our lives, they would teach us that we must marry someone who would make a great ministry team. This was not bad advice, but I know it was not the best teaching.

What happens in most cases is we have been brain washed into believing that our lives inside of the four walls of the church are more important that our lives outside of the church building. We only spend about five hours a week in church and the other one-hundred and sixty three hours are spent personally. Do not make the mistake of living for the church members over living for your own peace of mind.

My personal testimony is long. It is full of many instances where I dated someone just because of how good it would look for my ministry dreams. Just imagining how I and a few former mates would have looked standing in the pulpit together, preaching, singing, and praying for people was so alluring. Honestly, those that I did date and were committed to are highly anointed. So, based upon how I was taught, I automatically thought that each one must have been the one. I thought, I must be willing to commit to her so that we can do ministry together. Better yet, this would look good for church. We are both good looking. We are both anointed, and we are both on fire for God. That was how it appeared to be in front of the congregations. As I said before, that is only a few hours out of the week. As soon as you both get in the car, things can immediately change.

I have experienced having a mate that could sing, preach, and pray until Heaven shows up in the church; but as soon as service was over, they could raise Hell in a blink of an eye. Unfortunately, I was never taught that people know how to be anointed and powerful in the church house but they can still be full of evil. For those of you reading that have children, I would encourage you to never paint the church picture for your kids to make life decisions around it. I was really lost. I am in the middle of my twenties, preaching the gospel, serving as a minister in the Lord's church, and totally lost and confused. I was thinking that I made the best decision because I put ministry first and not my own life.

Do not allow yourself to get caught up with a fake church actor. These are the people who know how to do church behavior really well. They can front like they are so anointed and they are far from it. The truth be told, I was fooled because of my own slacking with prayer and fasting. I know that my intentions were good, but I began to get comfortable with the level of anointing on my life and I missed the voice of God. I was so concerned with finding a great teammate for church and not a great teammate for home. I even saw things in my mate that I knew were not going to work for my happiness, and I stayed in the relationship because I saw the potential to have a dynamic ministry together. That was not going to work.

You must also be careful when you share your heart with your potential mate. If you do not know their full motives, they can get a hold of your heart and act like the person that they know you want. If they know you have a heart for ministry, they will play the role of the dynamic ministry partner that you want for the entire dating period. If they are a fake, as soon as you make the full commitment, all of the acting goes down the drain. It is almost as if they say to themselves, "I got you now". This is when all of the church acting behavior gets frustrating because it is not really who they are. Fake people can't be fake forever. The real version of them has to eventually be revealed! Be extremely watchful of a person who is fake in church and real at home. Although it would also be trouble to have someone who is fake at home and real in church, a person who really is "crazy", is harder to deal with at home.

Know this: the people in your church do not have to deal with the mess that you are going to deal with if you marry who they think you look good with. They only see their gifts in action on the grand stage. Church members do not get to see the person's evil ways behind the scenes. All of the competition and the jealousy that comes with a couple that should make a great team in ministry is hardly ever revealed before a congregation. Normally, it is only one of the mates who has this hidden problem and over time it will slowly be revealed. But you will not see it publically in the beginning stages. It will manifest. It is nice to look good together. It better to actually be good together. Do not force yourself into a commitment just to satisfy the mirage of a power couple in church.

Bible Reference:

Mark 13:9 But take heed to yourselves: for they shall deliver you up to councils; and in the synagogues ye shall be beaten: and ye shall be brought before rulers and kings for my sake, for a testimony against them.

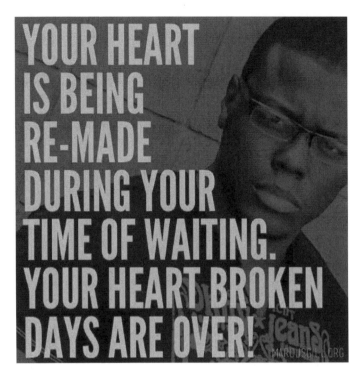

46

BRAND NEW HEART

Waiting is never a waste of your time or God's time. Please know that your time of waiting is being filled with healing. Those bad experiences that you have had with past relationships are being molded into your most powerful testimony. All of the broken pieces in your life are being put back together again. When God finally reveals His blessing for you, you will be able to enjoy it without the pain of being broken. God is fixing you up!

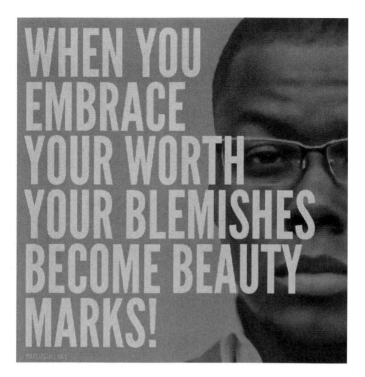

WHEN YOU EMBRACE YOUR WORTH YOUR BLEMISHES BECOME BEAUTY MARKS!

47

I LOOK GREAT!

God will most certainly give you beauty for your ashes! All of the rough things that messed you up are going to be used to set you up for greatness. Your scars are not to make you look bad. Your scars are a sign of how strong you really are. They are not blemishes. When you know your value everything about you (the good and the bad) turns into your greatest reason to shine. Chose beauty over blemishes!

YOUR HEART IS A TREASURE IT MAY HAVE BEEN BROKEN BUT NEVER DESTROYED

48

YOU OVERFLOW WITH VALUE.

It is not over for you. You may have thought so at one point and time in your life, but God is not finished with you yet! There are some things that break and you throw them away. Then there are other things that break, but you keep them because you know it has value. This is you. You may have been broken or beat in life, but God did not get rid of you. You are too valuable for the trash! You deserved to be fixed, shined, and ready for the best life.

LET GO OF THE TRASH OF YOUR PAST AND EMBRACE THE TREASURES OF YOUR FUTURE!

49

LET IT GO!

Stop holding on to so much mess. In order for you to move forward, you must release yourself from the weight of you trashy past. You may be so loving and so passionate for others; but, for you to truly be free and happy, you have to let go of those people that you know meant you no good. Love them from a distance and move on. You cannot walk in a new life carrying old baggage. Especially garbage bags! Let it go!

CONDUCT A FULL BACKGROUND CHECK ON YOUR POTENTIAL MATE BEFORE MAKING THE COMMITMENT OF GIVING THEM YOUR FULL LIFE!

50

RESEARCH!

It is sad to say, but taking somebody's word for who they are is not enough. You cannot trust people based on face value alone. Yes, they are saved. Yes, they love God; but, you better do a background check before you make any lifetime commitment. You need to check out their legal history. Research their medical history. Take a good look at their family. Find out their values.

You so not want to fall in love with someone and then be disappointed that you married a criminal. Yes, we all know that everyone has a past. I am not going to hate someone because they once were lost in a world of sin, but I refuse to commit to trouble. If you do not know your potential mate's background, you will be surprised with trouble. You will begin to discover things that will dishearten you. You should have proof of their education. You should check their credit. Nowadays, you can simply google a person's name and see if they have ever committed a major crime.

If your potential mate has had previous street life commitments, you do not want to be caught in the middle of that. The person in whom you are interested may have mental health issues. If you are unware of this, you will not know what is going on with their emotions at times. You need to know if they have ever been married before. You need to know if they have children. You should even know what their ex-mates look like.

Ask questions. Get to know their friends. Connect with family members. Talk about old times. Look at old pictures. Find out as much as you can before commitment. Do not get stuck in a bad relationship full of surprises! Do your intense research. You are better safe now than sorry later. Trust me, it is the most shocking and confusing feeling in the world to discover shameful secrets.

Marcus Gill is a yielded vessel to the will of God for his life. He has not only understood the will of God, but it has become the call on his life, to repair the breach, restore the old waste places, and lead the way to prosperity. His approach to ministry focuses on bridging the gap of cultures, ages, and society by offering a sound that is relative to every listener. He is chosen by God to do great works for a time such as this. His ministry is designed to reach lost souls and inspire believers.

By faith he believes that we all have been given a "license for victory" that can never be revoked.

He attended the Winston-Salem State University, where he perfected his knowledge in music business. He has also successfully completed certified coursework at Harvard University in the area of Religious Literacy.

He is in a season of his life where he is the author of 3 books entitled Single God Life, 10 Ways to Stay Free, Happy Single You and his latest release Psalm Saturday, he's a Charisma Magazine published author, he's been on numerous radio shows, and been interviewed on the internationally syndicated Turning Point broadcast on the Christian Broadcasting Network, TCT (Total Christian Television) and the Word Network.

Marcus is a world renowned, world traveling motivational speaker, preacher, and social media sage who has over 1.4 million followers on Facebook and is reaching MILLIONS of people each week.

29577188R00077

Printed in Great Britain
by Amazon